THE DIA BOOK
ABSOLUTES

From an Old Girl Cat and

Her Soul Brother Fa

by Robyn Lee

WITH ILLUSTRATIONS BY ROBYN LEE

BALBOA.
PRESS

A DIVISION OF HAY HOUSE

Balboa Press books may be ordered through booksellers or by contacting:

Balboa Press
A Division of Hay House
1663 Liberty Drive
Bloomington, IN 47403
www.balboapress.com
1 (877) 407-4847

Because of the dynamic nature of the Internet, any web addresses or links contained in this book may have changed since publication and may no longer be valid. The views expressed in this work are solely those of the author and do not necessarily reflect the views of the publisher, and the publisher hereby disclaims any responsibility for them.

The author of this book does not dispense medical advice or prescribe the use of any technique as a form of treatment for physical, emotional, or medical problems without the advice of a physician, either directly or indirectly. The intent of the author is only to offer information of a general nature to help you in your quest for emotional and spiritual well-being. In the event you use any of the information in this book for yourself, which is your constitutional right, the author and the publisher assume no responsibility for your actions.

Any people depicted in stock imagery provided by Getty Images are models, and such images are being used for illustrative purposes only. Certain stock imagery © Getty Images.

Print information available on the last page.

ISBN: 978-1-9822-0818-9 (sc)
ISBN: 978-1-9822-0819-6 (e)

Library of Congress Control Number: 2018908136

Balboa Press rev. date: 08/06/2018

My purpose
is to master the space
between me
and
the rest of the world.

— DIA THE CAT

Illustrations by Robyn Lee
Book design by Bekka Lindström
Author's photo by Laurent Ziegler Bildrecht

This book is set in the font Priori Serif from the Emigre Type Co. and includes ligatures in its character set. The use of ligatures in type design harkens all the way back to the Declaration of Independence.

Produced by Third Eye Media

OTHER BOOKS BY ROBYN LEE:

In The Moment: The Art of Being
Color Spa: Color Yourself In
The Book of TABs: Meditations on Acting Life

FOREWORD

Dia the cat was not fret-free and fuzzy. She was a spiritual anarchist who refused to be modified. Fa was her serious but clumsy student who grew to be master. Dia and her soul mate, Fa, followed the tradition of interspecies communications with slapstick, wisdom, unrelenting truth, and wild creativity.

Dia, a six-pound Siamese kitty, was a gift from a dear friend, Sally, who had hoped Dia would be a perfect studio cat – but instead of keeping mice away she set off the alarm. A year later Fa, a Siamese kitten was found in an Upper West Side Manhattan pet shop. We had been looking for a kitty just like him with his loud purr and promise of great size.

At a time when I was running in circles, chasing my own tail, Dia and Fa spoke up, engaging me in conversations which distracted me from myself just long enough for me to grasp some insights - some absolutes. The following are those conversations.

Dearest Dia, Welcome to my life. My house is yours. Let's take the tour. We have a circular loft: Come on, follow me ... This is the kitchen... into the bathroom and your box. Into the dining room ... into the lounge room and a fireplace that you are going to love! Into the extra room where I paint and our bedroom which leads back to the kitchen. And here's the roof garden! You can get out there from these windows. See all those plants? There's a lot to sniff out there. Dia I offer you absolute freedom.

**Absolute freedom?
That'll require
a lot of imagination.**

2.

Hi Dia. What have you been up to?

> **First, I bathed in the sun**
> **to separate body from mind,**
> **then I napped on the dirty**
> **clothes**
> **to anesthetize....**
> **then I got into the closet**
> **by the shoes in the back**
> **and I don't remember anything**
> **after that.**

That sounds like a lot! And it's only lunch
time.

3.

Whatcha doing, Dia?

**Waiting
for something
to happen.**

4.

**I like
that you see
the other world too.**

I like that you tolerate my moods.

5.

Look Dia, you've got a new brother and his
name is Fa!

Fa?

Dia this is Fa. Fa, this is Dia.

Hi. HI, HI!

He speaks!

And look! He's so tiny he fits into Nana's socks.
What do you think Dia?

**I think
one fur in the family
is enough!**

6.

I'm stuck. Got some advice for me Dia?

> **Listen
> for
> openings.**

> *... and there's chicken in humble pie.*

> **Another
> country
> heard from!**

7.

Can you read my mind?

**Can you
read
mine?**

Yes, I think so.

8.

I love getting wet under the tap.

I love to watch you enjoy yourself!

9.

No Dia! Don't do that! That's my armpit!
It's disgusting.

> **Someone's
> got to
> clean you up.**

10.

Hey! What's this fighting?

> **He**
> **took**
> **my spot.**

He's a baby! He doesn't know it's your spot.

> **Well he does now.**
> **This is mine.**
> **I was here first!**

So?

Dia was here first.

> **Look Fa, listen up.**
> **We have absolute freedom here**
> **but you have to ask me first.**

Ok.

You're a tough little girlie, Dia.

> **And**
> **don't you**
> **interfere.**

Ok. I guess you will have to work it out between you.
So... Who wants a treat?

> *Meeeee!*

> **Back off Fa!**
> **First in,**
> **first served.**

11.

Do you have faith, Dia?

> **I sleep**
> **with giants**
> **don't I?**

12.

What are you kitties doing?

**Transducing energy
from the cosmos
into real usable stuff.**

Well, whatever it is, it sure makes life sweeter.

13.

Hey Dia! You always look so peaceful. Like there's nothing on your mind. How do you do that?

**I outgrew
my
past.**

14.

Ok what do you two want now?

> **Aha Fa!**
> **The hairless kitty**
> **is open to suggestion!**
> **Let's imagine her**
> **giving us chicky**
> **on two little plates.**

How about chicky on two little plates?

> *She's getting better at this!*

> **And the great thing is,**
> **after this,**
> **we get to**
> **decide**
> **what we want**
> **next.**

15.

She has cheese!

Ok, hang on.
Here's the plan:
gently paw
head butt,
and purr.

You want some?

She softens to
appreciation.

16.

Where are you going, Dia?

Inside.

Whatcha going to do?

**Nothing's going on
so I'm going to bite
her toes.**

17.

Wanna come over here with me, Dia?

No.

Ok. Fa?

No.

Geez.

18.

Look at this mess. What am I going to do with
you two?

Nothing.

**We simply
have to be
endured.**

19.

Fafie, have you noticed that Dia always gets what she wants? How is that Dia?

> **I see life as a test
> of the strength
> of my resolve!**

It's a personal challenge, right?

> **My mind
> over
> your matter!**

20.

Dia, sometimes you guys look all lit up.
Energy shimmering all around you. It's almost
theatrical. Like the meeting of waters.

> **We let go of our bodies**
> **so our light**
> **can be seen.**

It's ... somehow enlightening.

21.

Go to sleep, Dia.

> **I can't sleep.**
> **Let me count the hairless beasts who love me.**
> **Robbie flaps I'm her near perfect cat,**
> **and Arley will attest to that!**
> **Daisy taught me how to purr.**
> **I'd preferably live with her!**
> **Carol's got a hot little head**
> **around which I make my bed.**

Come on, Dia. Settle down.

> **Lindy has a religious flare -**
> **she kisses red lipstick**
> **onto my forehead hair.**
> **Tod's still smoking**
> **and though we're not,**
> **we still enjoy a good chakra shock.**
> **Who else?**

Come on, Dia. Cuddle in here.

> **Grant's alternative life-style lap**
> **affords a kitty a spicy nap,**
> **and Maggie's close to cat.**
> **She runs, hides, and bites**
> **and stays up all night!**
> **Who else loves me?**

Come on. In here. That's a girlie, Dia. Right in
here.

> **Fafie, my dear soul mate**
> **and sounding board.**

That's a girl. Snuggle in.

> **Who else l o v e ' s ... y a w n**
> **loves meeeeeez**
> **e e e *zzzzzzzz*.**

22.

Dia! You're always bloody underfoot!

**That's a cruel description
of my devotion to you
in the kitchen.**

Sorry, Dia but I almost tripped.

**I am not responsible
for where you put
your feet!**

23.

Cunning little Dia. You've the face of an angel,
the mind of a snake, and a nose the size of a
garden pea.

**And
here
we sit.**

And here we sit. What's life all about, Dia?

**Life's about
you
and me.**

24.

Come over here. I need my kitties right now.

> **Misery**
> **loves**
> **cat company.**

You go.

> **Ok.**

What should I do? A decision has to be made but I can't make up my mind.

> **Wait**
> **for the answer**
> **to descend.**

You think wait? You're right. Let's get a cup of tea and wait together.

25.

Who are you guys really, Dia?

> **Behavioral modification devices.**

It's remarkable, but you keep me in a good mood.

26.

I don't know what to do today, Dia.

> **Do
> what occurs
> to you.**

On the fly, eh? Good idea!

27.

Fa is sorry
he jumped on that shelf
and broke all the glasses.

Oh, it was Fa, was it?

28.

Let me finish this first and then I'll get to your kitty needs. Ok?

> **That's
> a big
> ask.**

Can you back off for a bit? Give me some space!

> **Meow!**

Fifteen minutes.

> **Ten!**

Ok, ten.

> **You
> better get
> going then!**

29.

Dia, get down from that window ledge! You're on the very edge! You could fall off! Dia. You are always on the epi-edge of things - the stairs, the table, the bed. What's with this compulsion? Get down! Why do you do that?

> **When I'm on my pillow,
> I could be
> anywhere.**

Dia please!

> **When I'm on the edge,
> I really know
> where I am.**

Your call then.

30.

I'm confused!

Who?

31.

Look what I've got! Rum raisin ice cream,
cashew nuts, avocado dip and taco chips.
Popcorn, cheese and something hot: chicken
broccoli with garlic sauce.

**Something hot
would be
nice!**

Something hot!

Something hot would be nice.

32.

Whatcha thinking, Dia?

> **When I forget**
> **I love you**
> **treats turn sour.**
> **Which reminds me ...**
> **the dry food**
> **is down.**

Oh look, the dry food is down. Let me freshen
up your bowl.

33.

Grumpy, Dia?

She was smiling a lot and then she got a headache.

What brought that on?

Contrast.

34.

Who did this?

> *Dia.*

Dia. How can you miss the box? Now I have to clean this up. Gosh, Dia. What do you have to say for yourself? You know better than that.

> **Enlightenment's
> a
> spotty thing.**

35.

I've lost my little earring and I don't see it.

**Use your
other
eye.**

36.

You were sound asleep. How did you hear that chip drop onto the sofa?

Opportunity knocked.

37.

How do you guys always land on your feet?

> **We see**
> **what's coming**
> **before it gets here.**

38.

Get it, Dia. That's enough. You can't have any more!

**What?
Let me wrap my head
around that.**

Yeah, wrap your little head around that!

39.

You give me joy guaranteed.

40.

Tell Fa what happened with the dog downstairs.

> **One day that huge dog**
> **bolted up the stairs**
> **towards us.**

He came up here …

> **I seized**
> **the**
> **top step**

… she stared him down.

> **He**
> **slowly**
> **approached …**

They touched noses …

> **and**
> **he**
> **blinked.**

… and she hit him on the snout and he tumbled down.

> **I drowned**
> **his whimpering**
> **with my rage.**

Then she screamed like a warrior.

> **That's why**
> **he never**
> **comes up here.**

That's why he never comes up here.

> *Wow!*

41.

You're awfully close, Dia...

**I like the
hot air
from our noses.**

Oy.

42.

What's going on?

> **We're going to
> sit around
> and get ideas
> and then
> we'll
> do something.**
>
> *Great! I'm in.*

43.

You're planning something! Let me guess.
You're getting ready to chase Fa around the
garden through the kitchen around the living
room over the bed out that window across the
fire escape back to the garden - again and again,
right?

> **We'll
> be quiet
> about it.**

44.

Dia, please get off that painting and come over
here. Ok ... you can have some popcorn.

**Butter
and
salt.**

45.

Get off my paper, Dia. I'm trying to write. Why do you always do that?

> **You make the paper vibrate**
> **so it's great to sit on.**
> **You should try it.**

46.

Look what I've got! A battery vacuum cleaner for kitties!

NO!

Are you kidding? This is going to be fabulous!!

Is that a brush on the end?

Yup, there's a brush at this end... feel this!

Ooooooooooooooooohhhhhhhhhhhh

Brushing and pulling up every hair....

Oh geeeeeee...

How does that feel, Dia?

**Ooooooooooooohhh
ahhhhhhhhhhhhhpurr
aaaaaaaaahhhhhhhhhhh.**

Right? What do you think, Dia?

**I'd
line up
for that!**

47.

**When our whiskers grow
beyond our cheeks,
we're reaching
insight's peak.
With her it's her nose
and feet!**

48.

Stop that, Fa. Leave me alone. I mean it.

> **Fa, this is when you
> observe
> but don't get involved.**

49.

**What's
the
matter?**

I keep remembering that awful feeling.

**Then
why
remember?**

Right, why remember.

50.

Dia, come over here. Let's call Daisy. "Daisy, got a sec? Guess what Dia did in class today. Edmund was up and made a total mess of his monologue. I stopped him and he got angry and belligerent. He wouldn't let go of some contrived idea he had. Then Dia came out, walked right up to him and let out a long, wild, angry scream.

**Change
or
be changed.**

Edmund gasped for air, laughed, then cried. He did the monologue again. It was his best acting yet. Isn't that remarkable? By the end of class Edmund was glowing. Dia transformed him."

**If you don't
keep becoming
you become a cliché.**

51.

Dia, you are teaching me how to listen.

**And you are
teaching me
how to speak.**

52.

What are you guys doing speeding up and down
the spiral staircase?

> **Defying gravity.**
> **Relying on instinct.**
> **Challenging our character.**

You're very determined about it.

> **We're exercising**
> **our**
> **influence.**

You're so fast.

> *The faster we go the better it feels.*

Carry on then.

53.

What do you say, Dia?

**Evolution
is a promise
kept.**

54.

Whatcha been up to, Dia?

> **At dawn I jumped through the window**
> **and hit the deck sniffing,**
> **and that bird was there**
> **pecking at the wheatgrass.**
> **I pivoted slowly,**
> **tail balanced,**
> **lips retreated,**
> **saliva dripping,**
> **and just when my claws came out,**
> **I tripped over the lavender**
> **and saw that the chives**
> **looked so crisp ...**

She missed that bird again.

You missed that bird again!

I missed that bird again.

55.

Shit, Dia! What now?

> **Sometimes**
> **food is better eaten**
> **outside the bowl.**

What would your mother think about that?

> **My mother**
> **taught me not to care**
> **about what she thought.**

So, you don't care, eh? That's probably healthy.
Meanwhile what am I to do about this?

> **Clean it up**
> **or**
> **don't look.**

56.

What are you looking at from the top of the spiral stairs?

**The dimensions
of the life we have
together.**

57.

What's happening?

I'm spitting mad over what he did. Withholding my class money! It's outrageous. No. I can't give you any attention right now, kitties. I just can't get over it. I'm going to take him to small claims court. Leave me alone for a bit, ok? I said go! Go! ... ok. Ok. Come over here then.

**We survived
another
mixed message.**

58.

Jeez, Dia, what about her energy? It was dirty
grey green. It felt awful. She should tell the
truth. Her physical body will reflect her behav-
ior and she'll get really sick.

**It's none
of your
business.**

59.

That's a big jump you are eyeing, Fafie. You might give that a little think.

Dia said thinking restricts impulse.

60.

She's a fantastic choreographer. A genius!

**She is
echoing
source.**

61.

From the top of the door
I wait for Fa
to walk innocently by.

A tuft of hair floats to the floor
as we scurry away
from our fun.

62.

Remember when we thought that to survive, we had to control each other?

Yeah.
Now we just
nap.

63.

**I sit
on her chest
when she cries.**

You take the ride.

**So she knows
she's not
alone.**

64.

So, Dia, Fa, it turns out that we are complicated beings. We have a body, a mind that directs it, and a spirit that guides us. Who we really are instigates the actions of who we pretend to be.

**Then we should
keep an eye on
how we're acting.**

65.

Why do you do that, Dia? It's disgusting and just
not understandable.

> **I don't know why**
> **I pee in plastic bags.**
> **Let's just forget about it.**
> **I forget about**
> **a lot of things**
> **you do.**

66.

Dia! Fa! I got that great big Broadway show! I've
always wanted one. I've thought about it for
years so ... what does that teach us, Dia?

**To respect
our
thinking.**

67.

It's impossible.

> **You're
> looking
> for problems.**

Maybe I'm looking for problems.

68.

I keep bumping into things today, stubbing
my toes and dropping stuff. That drawer won't
close, the laundry won't fold, and my tape mea-
sure doesn't give me the same answer twice. I
have better things to do than fight with matter.

> **Matter**
> **has a mind**
> **of its own**
> **and deserves**
> **respect 'cause**
> **we walk on it,**
> **sit on it ,**
> **store things in it,**
> **and decorate it.**
> **Matter balances energy**
> **and protects us**
> **like a skin.**

Some days go really smoothly. But not today.

> **Matter holds our**
> **loft**
> **together**
> **and is not shy**
> **in revealing**
> **its consciousness.**
> **Matter loves**
> **co-creating.**
> **It can be**
> **heavy or**
> **weightless,**
> **comfortable or**

prickly,
faithfully mimicking
your mood –
and it shines
when you
love it.

You look so serious, Dia.

We speak kindly
to matter
'cause it softens
hard landings,
pops open cupboards,
and makes
wherever we nap
really
comfortable.

Well, I don't know what you just said but I think it was a mouthful! Haha heehee! Is the genius in the room speaking through kitty?

You
got
it!

So, I'm just going to lie down on the sofa and maybe nap. Wanna come with?

Thought
you'd never
ask.

69.

Gosh, Dia. I just can't win. Not up to par or something – not good enough - so what am I to do? Stop trying? I'm just not getting hired. Too old? Too … what? I am truly depressed. What am I going to do? I am ignorant and stupid in the corporate world, and I can't spell so proofing is out of the question.

> **Get off your back
> and
> on your side.**

Maybe I have to accept that who I am now no longer works commercially.

> **Sometimes opportunity
> looks
> like loss.**

Daisy says I should stop trying to fit in. Stop being conservative. That I should do like Voltaire said, cultivate my eccentricities. But what are they? I have a play I actually need to write. What do you think? Is it … time … to step up the creative ladder?

> **Would it make you happy?**

It would make me so happy.

> **Another
> problem
> solved!**

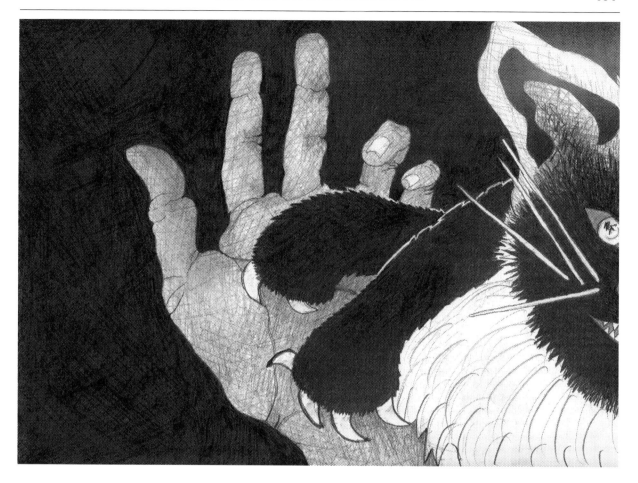

70.

We rumble tumble
then we
hold hands.

71.

You're such a good thinker, Dia!

> **I don't
> so much think
> as receive.**

72.

Then, happiness is the key?

Yes.
When we're happy
air bends,
time stretches,
and
matter yields.

The magic comes back.

The magic comes back
and we get
everything done.

And when it's over we snack and rest?

Right.

73.

It happened again. When will I learn?
What am I? An idiot? A glutton for punishment?
Her advice was good for her, but not for me.

> **Best
> to take
> your own advice.**

74.

How are you feeling today, Dia?

**More positive
than
negative.**

75.

What do you want, Dia?

> **I want
> to get
> into the closet.**

I'm thinking ... you want to go outside?

> **You can't hear me
> when you're
> thinking.**

Wanna snack?

> **I'll
> take
> it.**

76.

What are you waiting for, Dia?

> **The
> next
> question.**

77.

It didn't work out.

**Not
everything
does.**

78.

I love when the sun shines through that rose
quartz. ... What ideas will we tune in to today?
What color rocks? Ok. Let's take the yellow, the
green, and the red. Giving love with energy.

What are we doing?

**We're aligning
with
ideas.
We do it
as
a family.**

Oh.

79.

Dia come over here and let's call Carol. "Hi Carol, do you have a minute? Yes the play reading
went very well – eventually. It was hot in the the-
atre and by intermission everyone was sweating
and grumbling and some people left. When we
went back into the theater Dia was sitting center
stage. Totally magnetic, watching everyone get
back into their seats. I just let her be there. The
audience was delighted, giggling, and when the
actors came back to their chairs she walked off
to great applause. Dia saved the play!"

> **I lifted
> the mood
> of the room.**

"I think she did it on purpose."

She did.

80.

You're looking at me so intensely, Dia.

**I'm waiting
for you
to wake up.**

81.

Let me just get some water for you to sip before
I sit down.

> **You see?**
> **I don't have to speak**
> **to be heard.**

82.

Oh my ankle. I can barely walk. I don't want this. I have a big appointment today. Why did this happen?

> **Can't
> be
> explained.**

This is obvious physical evidence of my mis-alignment.

> **Or your path
> of least
> resistance.**

Though, in the back of my mind I was thinking I really didn't want to go.

> **So everything
> worked out
> for you.**

83.

Shall we go into the meditation room or stay out here?

**Doesn't matter.
We can plug in
anywhere.**

84.

I really want to embrace that idea. But how?

**Get up
to speed
with it.**

85.

When she turns over in bed, she hauls you over with
her. Doesn't that bother you?

It comforts her
so I
got used to it.

86.

What are you doing, kitty?

**Enjoying
my
sweet spot.**

87.

I'm bored.

**Then
turn
around.**

88.

Why did that happen to me? What was that?

> **Another
> enlightenment
> experience.**

89.

How do I have a better relationship with life?

**Understand
that you
create it.**

90.

Where was I?

> **Where
> you left
> yourself.**

Right.

91.

Dia what happened to Fafie?
His hairs are still up.

> **He squeezed**
> **under the fence**
> **and down the stairs**
> **into the garage.**
> **The door swung shut.**
> **Then he**
> **thought really hard**
> **about you**
> **and you found him.**

It was like I knew where he was.

**He'll
never do that
again.**

I'll never do that again.

92.

Seems I'm always dealing with something.

**Better than
something dealing
with you.**

93.

What should we do now?

**Let's
watch ideas
land.**

94.

We really communicate. Do you put your mind inside of mine, or am I putting mine inside of you?

> **We meet**
> **in the space**
> **between us.**

95.

Look at this bank statement. This is where we're at. What's going to turn this around?

> **The stream**
> **of**
> **life.**

96.

Hey you guys, time to meditate.

**Another
celestial
rendezvous!**

Relaxed, aware, devoted.

Relaxed, aware, devoted.

97.

What a good girl for not sitting on my black
sweater. Let's go outside for a brush.

**When you understand
the laws
of your universe,
life
gets
better.**

98.

**If she blames you
for what she hasn't done
walk away.**

99.

Whatcha doing, Fafie?

Keeping the ball in the air.

100.

Where's the inspiration? I've lost it and I'm
nothing without it.

> **It's**
> **up**
> **in the air.**
> **Just sit still**
> **so the goddess of wisdom**
> **can find you.**
>
> *And then just blurt it out!*

101.

How are you today, Dia?

Satisfied.

Me too.

102.

That's enough! Stop it!
You guys can be so disruptive.

**Disruptive
or
entertaining?**

You do make me laugh though.

103.

I really put my trust in that system. It gave me
such hope. Then the guy who created it was
discovered as being a tyrant and a rage-a-holic. I
actually don't know how to feel about it now.

**Create
a new
belief.**

104.

Words can't express how much I love you.

**We feel
what you
mean.**

105.

I don't know, I could do it, but is it a whim or an inspiration?

**Same
thing.**

106.

The going away bag is out!

Kitties, I have to go away for a while,

You can't go.

However, guess who's coming to stay with you?
Miss Julie!!!!

**When
do you
leave?**

107.

What do you say, Dia?

> **Live**
> **happily**
> **ever after.**

108.

What are you guys doing?

Watching energy speak.

What do you hear?

**Happiness
is the greatest
idea.**

109.

Dia, you don't speak English, but I hear words
from you.

> **You are**
> **translating**
> **my vibrations.**

110.

I'd describe myself as an introvert with an extrovert destiny. How would you describe yourself?

Hmm ... ?
Primitive
futurist.

111.

How do I get out of this rut?

> **Have
> a better
> idea.**

112.

It's all in how I see it, huh?

**I see
my bowl
as half full.**

Let me top off your bowl.

**... And
so
it is.**

113.

Hard to see isn't it, Dia? But you get around the house so well.

> **I know**
> **where**
> **I am.**

You're so clever following the wall to get every-where.

> **Sometimes**
> **the wall**
> **is the way.**

You always have great ideas, Dia.

> **I**
> **certainly**
> **do.**

114.

Fafie, stop that! Dia was sleeping. You're so
aggressive with her these days. You have to stop
spitting and batting at her. She doesn't feel well.

She should stop feeling sick!

I'm afraid of losing her too.

115.

There is so much wacky energy knocking
around.

**Let's
do
something.**

Let's do something!

116.

Oh, Dia! You've pulled the flowers out of the
vase again! Why do you do that?

    I
    love
    flowers.

117.

What would happen if I just said no to that job?

You'd
feel
better.

118.

Do you have some advice for me, Dia?

**Find light
and
sit in it.**

119.

Tough without Dia with us isn't it, Fa?

I can't sleep.

I know Fafie. You get up at all hours looking for
her. Crying for her. We have to get you eating
again, Fa. The vet says you've lost six pounds.
Dia's exact body weight.

I wanted to kill her.

...but you were too civilized for that!

120.

You know what I am doing, Fa?

      Feeding your feelings. Give me a little plate.

Let me give you a little plate.

121.

Look what I got, Fafie. Catnip from Sri Lanka!
And a real fur seal. I know it's not Dia. I just
want us to feel better. ... What would Dia say
right now?

That we came for the fun.

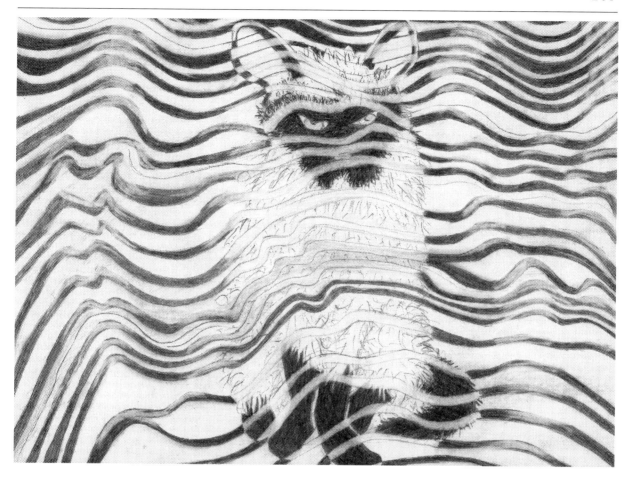

122.

There you are. You've been lost for three hours!
Where were you hiding?

    Behind the curtain.

My God, you were behind the curtain! How
do you do that? How do you disappear in plain
sight?

    I aim my cells away from the light and
    become a shadow.

Dia used to do that too. Well, I see you now. So,
let's have a snack.

123.

Do you think you should be sleeping under the covers? You're probably losing brain cells with the lack of oxygen.

It's my dream cave.

Up to you then.

124.

I found that feather we used to play with.

125.

Fa. Fa? Where are you? I'm leaving now. God.
Right in front of the tulips! You think this is
funny, right? Ok then. Food is in the bowl. See
you later! …

> *Ok. I'm going to eat, then play with that naughty rib-
> bon …*

And don't eat that ribbon!

> *… and then nap.*

I'll be home soon.

> *Ok.*

I feel we are having a bit more fun now.

> *We've accepted our lot.*

You are one terrifically loveable kitty! I am so
glad that we are here together.

> *Me too.*

126.

What was the biggest lesson Dia taught you?

To be a good sport.

I've learned to be a good sport.

127.

Fa … fa, you are such a fabulous kitty! You are
completely beautiful and huggable and wise. We
should write a book together about our life with
Dia. Re-create those conversations.

They've gathered momentum in me too.

We should talk to someone about it.

Don't poll the people.

Did you hear that?
Dia said don't poll the people.

Let's just get them down on paper.

128.

A letter from Dia arrived in my heart.

Have you heard from Dia?

> **"Dearest Robbie and Fafie,**
> **You are my**
> **dearest friends.**
> **I've**
> **got a great**
> **idea.**
> **Let wisdom**
> **drop from your heads**
> **to your lap**
> **and I'll meet you**
> **for a**
> **little nap."**

I really feel Dia here. Let's all have a little nap together.

129.

Oh, Fafie. What would Dia say about this little book?

She'd say it was great to sit on!

130.

Remember the cat prayer Dia taught us?

Let's sing it now:

Mee --- ow
.... Mee --- ow
Mee --- ow
.... Mee --- ow
Ahmen.

Printed in the United States
By Bookmasters